Compiled by
Kim Burnham

PETER PAUPER PRESS, INC.
WHITE PLAINS, NEW YORK

For my sister Suzanne,
a new Californian

Copyright © 1993
Peter Pauper Press, Inc.
202 Mamaroneck Avenue
White Plains, NY 10601
All rights reserved
ISBN 0-88088-768-0
Printed in Hong Kong
7 6 5 4 3 2 1

VINTAGE CALIFORNIA

"But how much is there of useful land?" questioned Senator Daniel Webster in 1850, during the debate on admitting California to the Union. In fact, California, with its majestic landscape, agricultural riches, and glamor, has proved itself to be truly the "Golden State."

California has often represented the American

Dream—both to 19th Century gold-rushers and to the adoring fans of today's Hollywood movie stars. So why not read through this book, and learn how California has touched its sons and daughters as well as its critics.

*   *   *   *

The birthplace of each Californian quoted is

noted below the name. Where no birthplace appears, it is believed that the person quoted was not California born or the birthplace is not known.

VINTAGE CALIFORNIA

I attended a dinner the other morning given for the Old Settlers of California. No one was allowed to attend unless he had been in the State 2 and one half years.

WILL ROGERS

VINTAGE CALIFORNIA

*T*here are a lot of blessings
in Napa Valley. It's a
simple but gracious way of
life.

ROBERT MONDAVI

VINTAGE CALIFORNIA

I came out here with one suit and everybody said I looked like a bum. Twenty years later Marlon Brando came out with only a sweatshirt and the town drooled over him. That shows how much Hollywood has progressed.

HUMPHREY BOGART

*T*his city [San Francisco] typifies the American dream of a sense of tolerance and openness, with different people living closely together, carefully, with respect for the law, not impinging their will on others but living with a growing mutual respect.

DIANNE FEINSTEIN,
San Francisco

VINTAGE CALIFORNIA

*E*ureka. (I have found it.)

State Motto

VINTAGE CALIFORNIA

Then, ho, brothers, ho
To California go;
There's plenty of gold
  in the world we're told
On the banks of the
  Sacramento.

JESSE HUTCHINSON, JR.
Ho for California

VINTAGE CALIFORNIA

*T*he West Coast's gift to the world is an ever-growing range of interesting wines, both of bottles to try out against European classics and also some that are unlike anything else.

CHRIS FOULKES

*T*he whole world is looking east. To the Orient—to the future. That's why I love California. It's so close to China.

DIANA VREELAND

*W*hat was the use of my having come from Oakland it was not natural to have come from there yes write about it if I like or anything if I like but not there, there is no there there.

GERTRUDE STEIN

*T*he San Francisco Bay
Area [is] the playpen of
countercultures.

R. Z. SHEPPARD

VINTAGE CALIFORNIA

*I*n the luxuriance of a bowl of grapes set out in ritual display, in a bottle of wine, the soil and sunshine of California reached millions for whom that distant place would henceforth be envisioned as a sun-graced land resplendent with the goodness of the fruitful earth.

KEVIN STARR

VINTAGE CALIFORNIA

A ball player's got to be kept hungry to become a big leaguer. That's why no boy from a rich family ever made the big leagues.

JOE DIMAGGIO,
Martinez

VINTAGE CALIFORNIA

*H*ollywood is an extraordinary kind of temporary place.

JOHN SCHLESINGER

VINTAGE CALIFORNIA

*A*ny man who makes a
trip by land to California
deserves to find a fortune.

ALONZO DELANO,
in 1849

VINTAGE CALIFORNIA

*L*iving in California adds
ten years to a man's life.
And those extra ten years
I'd like to spend in New
York.

HARRY RUBY

VINTAGE CALIFORNIA

I believe that God felt sorry for actors so He created Hollywood to give them a place in the sun and a swimming pool. The price they had to pay was to surrender their talent.

SIR CEDRIC HARDWICKE

San Francisco is a mad city—inhabited for the most part by perfectly insane people whose women are of a remarkable beauty.

RUDYARD KIPLING

VINTAGE CALIFORNIA

I went out there for a thousand a week, and I worked Monday, and I got fired Wednesday. The guy that hired me was out of town Tuesday.

NELSON ALGREN

VINTAGE CALIFORNIA

*I*f you ever tilted the map
of the U.S.A. very sharply,
Los Angeles is the spot
where everything would
spill out.

FRANK LLOYD WRIGHT

VINTAGE CALIFORNIA

*T*oo many freeways, too much sun, too much abnormality taken normally, too many pink stucco houses and pink stucco consciences.

CLANCY SIGAL

VINTAGE CALIFORNIA

*E*very California girl has
lost at least one ovary and
none of them has read
Madame Bovary.

F. SCOTT FITZGERALD

Q. How many Californians does it take to change a light bulb?

A. Six. One to change the bulb and five to share the experience.

ANONYMOUS

VINTAGE CALIFORNIA

*C*alifornia is a queer place—in a way, it has turned its back on the world, and looks into the void Pacific.

D. H. LAWRENCE

VINTAGE CALIFORNIA

*W*hatever starts in California unfortunately has an inclination to spread.

JIMMY CARTER

VINTAGE CALIFORNIA

Sunny nutland.

EDWIN DIAMOND

VINTAGE CALIFORNIA

*T*he Senator says the territory of California is three times greater than the average extent of the new States of the Union. Well, Sir, suppose it is. We all know that it has more than three times as many mountains, inaccessible and rocky hills, and sandy wastes, as are possessed by any State of the Union. But how much is there of useful land? How much that may be made to contribute to the support of man and of society? These ought to be the questions. Well, with respect to that, I am sure that everybody has become satisfied that, although California may have a very great sea-board, and a large city or two, yet that the agricultural

VINTAGE CALIFORNIA

products of the whole surface now are not, and never will be, equal to one half part of those of the State of Illinois; no, nor yet a fourth, or perhaps a tenth part.

DANIEL WEBSTER,
in 1850

VINTAGE CALIFORNIA

*T*he attraction and superiority of California are in its days. It has better days, and more of them, than any other country.

RALPH WALDO EMERSON

. . . *t*he freeway experience . . . is the only secular communion Los Angeles has. . . . Actual participation requires a total surrender, a concentration so intense as to seem a kind of narcosis, a rapture-of-the-freeway.

JOAN DIDION,
Sacramento

VINTAGE CALIFORNIA

The art of Southern California finds its impetus in Zen and Jung, while Northern California is oriented toward Sturm und Drang.

HENRY HOPKINS

VINTAGE CALIFORNIA

*T*he California climate
makes the sick well and
the well sick, the old young
and the young old.

ANONYMOUS

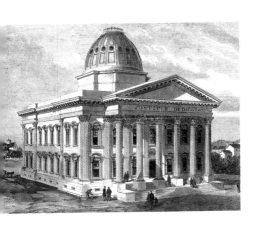

I'm not really a Hollywood person. Not that I don't like L. A. , but I'm just a Northern California guy.

CLINT EASTWOOD,
San Francisco

At half-past two o'clock . . .
I was awakened by a
tremendous earthquake . . .
the strange thrilling motion
could not be mistaken, and
I ran out of my cabin, both
glad and frightened,
shouting, "A noble earth-
quake! A noble earthquake!"
feeling sure I was going to
learn something.

JOHN MUIR, *in 1872*

VINTAGE CALIFORNIA

*T*he coldest winter I ever spent was a summer in San Francisco.

MARK TWAIN

VINTAGE CALIFORNIA

I made my mistakes, but in all my years of public life I have never profited, *never* profited from public service. I have earned every cent. . . . people have got to know whether or not their President is a crook. Well, I'm not a crook.

RICHARD M. NIXON,
Yorba Linda

VINTAGE CALIFORNIA

I can't deny the fact that
you like me! You like me!

SALLY FIELD,
Pasadena

VINTAGE CALIFORNIA

I injected life into the
city's tired bloodstream.
Apathy was replaced with
energy.... Palm Springs is
alive.

SONNY BONO,
Mayor of Palm Springs

VINTAGE CALIFORNIA

California is the only state in the union where you can fall asleep under a rose bush in full bloom and freeze to death.

W. C. FIELDS

VINTAGE CALIFORNIA

*A*lcatraz, the federal prison with a name like the blare of a trombone, [is] a black molar in the jawbone of the nation's prison system.

THOMAS E. GADDIS

VINTAGE CALIFORNIA

California is a fine place to live in—if you happen to be an orange.

FRED ALLEN

VINTAGE CALIFORNIA

*M*y first wave was so insane . . . This wave was psycho it was so beautiful. I came off the bottom into this section and did this semi-soul arch little flash and just put my arms out on both sides, just arching back and going "Oh my gosh. This place is heaven."

PAT O'CONNELL

VINTAGE CALIFORNIA

Yosemite Valley, to me, is
always a sunrise, a glitter of
green and golden wonder
in a vast edifice of stone
and space.

ANSEL ADAMS,
San Francisco

VINTAGE CALIFORNIA

*T*he calamity which has
struck San Francisco has
had an echo in the hearts
of the people of the entire
world. . . . Nevertheless
. . . like the phoenix,
San Francisco will rise
again from the ashes,
greater, more beautiful,
and stronger.

SARAH BERNHARDT

*T*he Mojave is a big
desert and a frightening
one. It's as though nature
tested a man for endurance
and constancy to prove
whether he was good
enough to get to California.

JOHN STEINBECK,
Travels with Charley,
Salinas

VINTAGE CALIFORNIA

When I first came here
from England, I just came
on a hunch that I would
love it. I think it was partly
the sensuality, the sexiness,
and then, ultimately, its
spaciousness. It's a horizontal city, isn't it, Los
Angeles? Everything in
California is horizontal.

DAVID HOCKNEY

*E*ast is East, and West is San Francisco, according to Californians. Californians are a race of people; they are not merely inhabitants of a State.

O. HENRY

*T*he land around San Juan Capistrano is the pocket where the Creator keeps all his treasures. Anything will grow there, from wheat and beans to citrus fruit.

FRANCES MARION

VINTAGE CALIFORNIA

I remain California-bound ... I've got the telegram worn to a frazzle.

RONALD REAGAN

VINTAGE CALIFORNIA

*W*ars may be fought with weapons, but they are won by men. It is the spirit of the men who follow and of the man who leads that gains the victory.

GEORGE S. PATTON,
San Gabriel

*W*hat is sauce for the goose may be sauce for the gander, but is not necessarily sauce for the chicken, the duck, the turkey or the guinea hen.

ALICE B. TOKLAS,
San Francisco

VINTAGE CALIFORNIA

*P*eople, I just want to
say . . . can we all get along?
Can we get along? . . .
We've got enough smog
here in Los Angeles, let
alone to deal with the
setting of these fires and
things. . . . We're all stuck
here for a while. . . . Let's
try to work it out. . . . Let's
try to work it out.

RODNEY KING

*V*esuvius, sì; San Francisco, no!

ENRICO CARUSO

VINTAGE CALIFORNIA

I've been on a calendar,
but never on time.

MARILYN MONROE,
Los Angeles

I don't think that
California is a healthy
place.... Things disin-
tegrate there.

JOYCE CAROL OATES

VINTAGE CALIFORNIA

I class myself with Rin Tin Tin. At the end of the Depression, people were perhaps looking for something to cheer them up. They fell in love with a dog, and with a little girl. . . . I think it won't happen again.

SHIRLEY TEMPLE,
Santa Monica

VINTAGE CALIFORNIA

*T*his valley [Yosemite] is the only place that comes up to the brag about it, and exceeds it.

RALPH WALDO EMERSON

VINTAGE CALIFORNIA

I am a pilgrim, a pilgrim and a mediante from California I came—there as a child I played in the meadows. California is the land of gold—not therefore the gold which is coined in money but the free glad gold of the orange and the California poppy.

ISADORA DUNCAN,
San Francisco

*P*eople in Hollywood
can't face the truth in
themselves or in others.
This town is filled with
people who make adventure
pictures and who have
never left this place. . . .
They make pictures about
love and they haven't been
in love—ever.

RICHARD BROOKS

*T*he Bay Area Tradition represents not a style, but a process of synthesis and transformation: a design approach with trademarks and no rules.

JOHN BEACH

VINTAGE CALIFORNIA

*T*here had been a time when they had thought Berkeley wasn't the real world. Many, like Susie, who had left to find the real world when the Movement and their marriages fell apart were returning.

SARA DAVIDSON,
Loose Change:
Three Women of the Sixties

VINTAGE CALIFORNIA

*I*f a man comes to
California and stays two
years, he will never want to
leave it.

JAMES CARSON

VINTAGE CALIFORNIA

*B*rave golden California,
more brave and golden for
such possibilities surely,
than any other country
under the sun!

HENRY JAMES

I set out to create the most exciting team in the world. And, by doing that, cement a relationship between the city of Los Angeles and the Lakers as Berry Gordy had done with Detroit and Motown.

DR. JERRY BUSS

VINTAGE CALIFORNIA

*l*ater dude!

DINO ANDINO,
California surfer